**This book is to be returned on or before
the last date stamped below.**

10 FEB 1999

14 FEB 2000

1 0 FEB 2011

9017

DISCOVERING SACRED TEXTS

Series editor:
W. Owen Cole

The Guru Granth Sahib

Piara Singh Sambhi

HEINEMANN

Heinemann Library
an imprint of Heinemann Publishers (Oxford) Ltd
Halley Court, Jordan Hill, Oxford OX2 8EJ

OXFORD LONDON EDINBURGH
MADRID ATHENS BOLOGNA PARIS
MELBOURNE SYDNEY AUCKLAND SINGAPORE
TOKYO IBADAN NAIROBI HARARE
GABORONE PORTSMOUTH NH (USA)

First published 1994

**A catalogue record for this book is
available from the British Library**

ISBN 0 431 07370 8
98 97 96 95 94
10 9 8 7 6 5 4 3 2

Designed and produced by Visual Image,Street
Cover design by Philip Parkhouse, Abingdon
Produced by Mandarin Offset
Printed and bound in Hong Kong

Introduction to the series

The purpose of these books is to show what the scriptures of the six religions in the series are, to tell the story of how they grew into their present form, and to give some idea of how they are used and what they mean to believers. It is hoped that readers will be able to appreciate how important the sacred texts are to those who base their lives on them and use them to develop their faith as well as their knowledge. For this reason, members of the six major religions found in Britain today have been asked to write these books.

W. Owen Cole (Series Editor)

Dedication

This book is dedicated by Piara Singh Sambhi to Professor Bakshish Singh, a learned Sikh well versed in his scriptures and a wise and reliable friend.

Acknowledgements

Piara Singh Sambhi provided all the material upon which this book is based and read the original draft of it before he died. It was completed and seen through to publication by the Series Editor, who would like to thank Jaswant Singh Sambhi and his mother for their kindness and support and approval of the book in its final form, and Professor Bakshish Singh for his immense support and help and especially for reading through and approving the final text. In the circumstances a more than usual burden has fallen upon Sue Walton, Tristan Boyer and Alison Sims of Heinemann. It is hoped that the resulting publication is one which does as much justice as any can to a fine Sikh and much loved and respected friend.

We are grateful to Mrs Mansukhani for permission to use material from *Hymns from the Dasam Granth* and the *Hymns from the Bhai Gurdas's Compositions* translated by her late husband, the famous scholar Dr G. S. Mansukhani, and published by Hemkunt Press, India, on pp. 9, 13, 21, 23, 25, 29, 31, 43, 47.

The Publishers would like to thank the following for permission to reproduce photographs: W. Owen Cole pp.4, 7, 15, 20, 22, 26, 29, 30, 32, 40, 44, 45, 46, 47; J. Kalidas p.38; Eluned Lyons p.41; Harjinder Singh Sagoo pp.9, 10, 12, 14, 16, 24, 33, 35, 36, 37, 42.

The Publishers would like to thank the Hutchison Library (scripture) and Impact Photos/Christopher Cormack (granthi and children reading the Guru Granth Sahib) for the cover photographs.

Contents

1 The Guru Granth Sahib in worship

This unit tells you how Sikhs look after their most important religious book, the **Guru** Granth Sahib, during worship.

The Guru Granth Sahib in the gurdwara

The Sikhs' religious book, the Guru Granth Sahib, is so important that it is placed where everyone can see it in the Sikh place of worship called a gurdwara. If you were to enter a gurdwara the first thing that you would notice is the Guru Granth Sahib. It is the focal point, the object which everyone faces. It is placed upon a **manji sahib**, which looks rather like a throne, and has a canopy over it. Someone always sits or stands behind it holding a **chauri**. This is a fan made of peacock feathers, yak hairs or nylon. The fan isn't used to keep the Guru Granth Sahib cool! It is to show respect. Rulers of eastern countries often have an attendant who stands at their side holding something resembling the chauri. Someone may also hold an umbrella over their heads. Outside this may keep off the rain or protect them from the sun, but it might also be used on a dull or dry day, or inside a building. Like the canopy over the royal throne at state openings of the British Parliament, it is a symbol of sovereignty. It shows that the monarch is a special person. The canopy over the Guru Granth Sahib is used to show how important it is. Sikhs call it a **chanani**.

Other ways of respecting the Guru Granth Sahib

Sikhs also show respect for the Guru Granth Sahib in a number of other ways. They will bathe before going to the gurdwara to make sure that they are as clean as possible. When they enter the gurdwara they will take off their shoes. Any men who do not wear turbans will cover their heads in some way, perhaps with handkerchiefs, and women will use head scarves. Sikhs will kneel and bow in front of the Guru Granth Sahib till their foreheads touch the ground. They will make an offering. This is likely to be money but it may be a bottle of milk, some fruit, or flour to be used in preparing a meal which they will all share.

A Sikh woman reading the Guru Granth Sahib in a gurdwara. In Sikhism women and men are equal. There are no clergy or priests.

Worshippers will then find a space and sit cross-legged on the floor, taking care not to turn their backs to the Guru Granth Sahib as they do so. They will avoid sitting with their feet pointing towards the scripture because in Indian culture this is considered to be rude behaviour. Everyone is equal in Sikh eyes so there are no special places for important visitors or worshippers

like kings or prime ministers. Everyone sits at the feet of the scripture.

More than a book

The Guru Granth Sahib is more than a book. It is scripture, but it is treated in this particular way because it is the living word of God. Sikhs believe that the message which the gurus taught is not a dead letter belonging to the past.

When people visit our homes we expect them to respect our way of life. If you visit a gurdwara you must remove your shoes, cover your head, and leave anything containing tobacco outside.

Pictures

Palki

Reader, perhaps holding chauri

Guru Granth Sahib

Karah parshad in metal bowl

Ragis

Money offerings

Takht

Manji Sahib (stool) on which the Guru Granth Sahib is placed

Offerings of milk, fruit, etc.

Diagram of a gurdwara.

NEW WORDS

Chanani the canopy over the Guru Granth Sahib

Chauri the fan waved over the Guru Granth Sahib. It should never be called a 'fly whisk'

Guru spiritual teacher and guide

Manji sahib stool on which the Guru Granth Sahib is placed

As Sikhs enter God's house, the gurdwara, they may call God to mind with these words.
'Where does God live? Who will point me to the door which I have looked for, my heart turned from the world?'
'How can I cross life's ocean? How may I die to the world?'
'Suffering is the door to human life, violence the door keeper, hope and anxiety the door posts. This house is founded upon illusion. Truth alone provides security.'
'God's many names do not reveal God's greatness. No one is God's equal. Humanity has no reason to boast. We must live humbly.' (Guru Nanak: AG 877)

2 Caring for the Guru Granth Sahib

This unit describes the way Sikhs look after the Guru Granth Sahib when it is not in use.

The Guru Granth Sahib is far too important to be left unattended in the gurdwara. Whenever it is open someone will be sitting behind it. At night when everyone goes to sleep it is laid to rest as well.

Sukhasan

There is a special ceremony which takes place every day in every gurdwara. It is called **Sukhasan**. Many Sikhs try to be in the gurdwara to take part in it but really only two or three are necessary.

One Sikh reads the hymn, **Kirtan Sohila**, the Song of Praise, which all Sikhs should use as a prayer before going to sleep. Here is one of its five verses:

> 'We are gathered to worship and praise God and ponder on God's name. Sing the glory, reflect on the wonders of the One who is Ruler and Protector of all things.
>
> All must receive their last call from God. Daily those souls who must go are summoned. Keep in mind the One who will summon you. Soon you will hear the command.
>
> There are six great traditions (in Hindu teaching), each with its master, doctrines and faith. Yet there is only One God who is the Guru of gurus and Teacher of everyone.
>
> Seconds and minutes, hours, days and seasons all recognize one source. Just as they spring from their creator, the sun, so all that exists comes from God.
>
> Worldly souls who scorn God's sweetness suffer pain because of their conceit. The thorn of death pricks deeper and deeper. Those who love God's sacred name shall break the bonds of birth and death. Thus they find the eternal One; thus they win supreme honour. I am poor and humble; keep and

> save me, God most high. Grant the aid that your name can give me. Grant me the peace and joy. Grant the joy of serving all who praise God's name.'

Someone then says a special prayer while the rest stand. The scripture is then closed and wrapped in some clothes called **rumalas**. The attendant puts another rumala on his or her head. This is worn on top of her head scarf in the case of a woman, or on his turban if the attendant is a man. Then the Guru Granth Sahib is lifted up, put on the attendant's head and carried to where it will be placed for the night. This is usually a bed in another part of the gurdwara. As it is taken to its resting place someone will walk behind it holding a chauri, and all the people present will turn towards it and bow as it is carried past them. Then they will form a procession and follow it chanting these words:

> 'Wherever my true Guru goes to stay, that place is blessed. The Guru's Sikhs find that place and apply its dust to their heads. The efforts of the Guru's Sikhs have succeeded. Those who meditate on God, those who venerate their True Guru, eventually become respected themselves by the grace of God.'

Parkash Karna

Early in the morning, perhaps as soon as four o'clock, a ceremony which is the complete reverse of Sukhasan is performed. This is **Parkash Karna**. A group of Sikhs, who have previously bathed, carry the Guru Granth Sahib from its overnight resting place to its throne in the gurdwara, the manji sahib. The wrappings which were used at Sukhasan are replaced with clean rumalas. While this is being done the worshippers sing hymns. Part of one reads:

> 'When I come into your presence I feel love. My hopes are fulfilled by your grace. Hear my request for the gift of being able to meditate on you and be your disciple. God, my true friend, listen to my prayer which is that you

The Guru Granth Sahib being carried to its overnight resting place at the Golden Temple, Amritsar. Note the attitudes of the devotees.

should remain in my heart forever. May I never forget you, the treasure house of every virtue.' (GGS 741.)

The **Ardas** congregational prayer is offered and then the scripture is opened at random and the first verse on the left hand page is read to the Sikhs who are present. This is called a **vak** and is regarded as the word of guidance for the day. As almost every sentence in the Guru Granth Sahib has a spiritual message there is no chance of the verse referring to something commonplace.

Many of the Sikhs then leave to begin their daily work. The vak is written on a notice board and read by the steady stream of Sikhs who come to the gurdwara throughout the day.

NEW WORDS

Ardas a special prayer used on all important occasions

Kirtan Sohila one of the hymns used before going to bed and at funerals

Parkash Karna ceremony of installing the Guru Granth Sahib

Rumala the cloth used for covering the Guru Granth Sahib when it is not being read

Sukhasan the ceremony of laying the Guru Granth Sahib to rest

Vak the message received after opening the scripture at random

Some words from Ardas.
'Grant your Sikhs a true knowledge of their faith, the blessing of uncut hair, guidance in behaviour, spiritual insight, patient trust and abiding faith, the supreme gift of the Divine Name (in their hearts). May all bathe in the sacred waters of Amritsar. May your eternal blessing rest on all who sing your praises, on the banners which proclaim your presence, and on all places which shelter and sustain your people. Let us praise the way of truth and call on God, saying Vahiguru! (The wonderful One – the popular name Sikhs use when addressing God.)'

3 Guru Nanak

This unit introduces the man who was the founder of the Sikh religion, Guru Nanak.

Guru Nanak was born in 1469, just over 500 years ago. A Guru is an Indian religious teacher who helps men and women to know God and helps them with any personal problems they may have. People who become the followers of such a teacher are called disciples. This is what the Punjabi word Sikh means.

Guru Nanak was born in north west India, in a region called Punjab. It was about the same size as England but today part of it is in Pakistan and the rest is in India. Guru Nanak taught in Punjabi. This explains why Punjabi is the special language of the Guru Granth Sahib. There were ten Sikh gurus altogether. Their names were:

1 Guru Nanak: born 1469, died 1539.
2 Guru Angad: born 1504, died 1552.
3 Guru Amar Das: born 1479, died 1574.
4 Guru Ram Das: born 1534, died 1581.
5 Guru Arjan: born 1563, died 1606.
6 Guru Hargobind: born 1595, died 1644.
7 Guru Har Rai: born 1630, died 1661.
8 Guru Har Krishan: born 1656, died 1664.
9 Guru Tegh Bahadur: born 1621, died 1675.
10 Guru Gobind Singh: born 1666, died 1708.

The first five Gurus and the ninth wrote hymns which are in the Guru Granth Sahib. The hymns of the tenth Guru are contained in another book.

The Gurus were important because they were the men through whom God's message was given. They always taught that the real Guru was God. The words which they passed on from God to people who would listen to them were eventually collected in one book, the Guru Granth Sahib. Sahib means master or lord. An Indian who wished to be respectful to his employer might address him as 'sahib'. Granth means collection, or book, so the title of the Sikh scripture, Guru Granth Sahib, can be translated as 'The collection of the teachings of the Lord God'. In Punjabi this is 'Sri Guru Granth Sahib Ji'.

Sikhs sit on the ground to sing hymns, as most Indians do, whatever their religion. They have a special reason for doing this. Symbolically they are sitting at the feet of their teacher. It also shows that they are all equal. No one is more important than anyone else.

Guru Nanak's sister, Nanaki, was the first person to recognise her brother's mission to preach God's word. She gave Mardana money to buy the rebeck instrument which he used to accompany Guru Nanak's hymns.

Guru Arjan describing God's love.
'When someone is in extreme difficulty with none to help, with friends who have become enemies and deserted by kin, when all support and hope has been lost, remember the Supreme One and then no harm shall come. God is the strength of the weak.'   (AG 70)

4 God's revelations to Guru Nanak

This unit tells you why Sikhs respect Guru Nanak so much.

Gurus can help people to know God because they know God themselves. Sikhs and many Hindus believe that God is present in all human beings. Most of us, however, are ignorant of this so we search everywhere else except the right place. Guru Nanak saw people leaving their families to live on their own in the forests or in caves on mountains. Others went thousands of miles to the source of the sacred River Ganges to bathe there. If they were sincere and already knew God their pilgrimages and **asceticism** might help them, but if they hadn't become aware of God within them these actions would not help.

Gurus are not self-appointed men or women (most are men). They don't wake up one morning or listen to a Guru and say 'I'm going to be a Guru when I grow up'. They are Gurus because they believe that God has called them to become Gurus.

The calling of Guru Nanak

Nanak was a very religious young man. He enjoyed talking with religious teachers about the meaning of life. He became aware of God at a very young age and spent much of his time in meditation. This meant concentrating his mind on thoughts of God. He trained himself to do it for hours at a time. But he was not yet Guru Nanak. He knew God but God had not yet told him to preach to other people.

One day, when he was about 30 years old, married with two sons, and employed as an accountant, he received his call. He went to bathe in the river as most Indians did each day, and he disappeared. A three-day search brought no trace of him. He must have drowned. To everyone's delight Nanak returned, but they were worried when he

remained silent in reply to all the questions they asked him. When Nanak did speak he told them that he had been taken to God's court and given the task of preaching God's message to the world. He was now Guru Nanak.

These are some words which he composed to describe his experience:

> 'I was a minstrel out of work.
> I became attached to divine service.
> The Almighty One commissioned me,
> "Night and day sing my praise".
> The master summoned the minstrel
> To the High Court, and robed me with the clothes of honour,
> To sing God's praises. Since then God's name has become the comfort of my life.
>
> 'Those who at the Guru's bidding feast and take their fill of the food which God gives, enjoy peace.
> Your minstrel spreads your glory by singing your word.
> By praising God, Nanak has found the Perfect One.'   (AG 150.)

Guru Nanak might easily have become a proud man. The crowds who came to listen to him and to become his disciples could have turned his head. However, he remained humble. He called himself 'Nanak Das', Nanak the slave of God. When someone

Guru Nanak with his companions, Bala, a Hindu, and the Muslim Mardana.

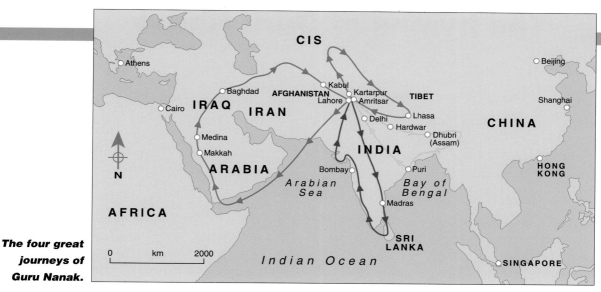

The four great journeys of Guru Nanak.

questioned him he said that he had no teaching of his own:

> 'I have no words of my own; as the word of God comes to me, so I speak it.' (AG 722.)

Guru Nanak put the teaching that he was given into poetry. Poetry is easier to remember than prose, which is what we usually speak. A Muslim friend, Mardana, from Guru Nanak's village, often travelled with him to provide music. Their journeys took them to many lands.

One day Guru Nanak and Mardana had the misfortune to be made prisoners of the Emperor Babur, whose army was conquering Punjab. An officer gave Mardana the job of looking after his horse. Guru Nanak felt that God was about to give him a message for the other prisoners so he told Mardana to be ready to play. Mardana didn't think this very wise. The horse might bolt and the soldier might kill Mardana for his neglect. Guru Nanak ordered him to let go of the horse because 'the word is descending'. The words which Guru Nanak then sang were not pleasant ones. He told the suffering prisoners that Babur would conquer the country and that the people were in trouble because they were not obeying God. They had been selfish while they were rich. They had ignored the poor; now they were poor themselves. Perhaps, though, now that they had lost everything they might turn to God.

NEW WORD

Asceticism a very strict lifestyle based on little food and drink and being unmarried

From the Japji, Guru Nanak's most famous composition, meditated upon daily.
'God can never be known through ritual purification though one cleanses oneself a thousand times. Silent reflection will never reveal God though one becomes absorbed in the deepest meditation. One may gather vast riches but hunger will remain. No cunning will help in the hereafter. How is truth to be attained and falsehood torn aside? Nanak says: Submit to God's order (hukam), walk in its way. God's Order is beyond description, though everything that exists is its visual expression. All forms of life are created by it, and it alone determines greatness. Some are raised up, others brought low, some must suffer while others find joy. Some receive blessing, others condemnation, doomed to transmigrate by God's order. All are within its power, none is beyond it. Those who comprehend it, Nanak says, renounce their blind self-centred pride.' (AG1)

5 The hymns of Guru Nanak

This unit is about some of Guru Nanak's experiences.

Guru Nanak travelled far and wide from about the year 1500 for some 20 years. His Muslim friend Mardana usually went with him. He visited the great cities of India such as Delhi and Varanasi (sometimes known as Benares), as well as Tibet, Sri Lanka, Iraq and the Muslim holy city of Makkah in Arabia. As he travelled he taught people the message which he had received from God. Sometimes his travels led him and Mardana into danger.

Guru Nanak at the home of a poor carpenter, Bhai Lalo, who became a Sikh. Guru Nanak preferred to stay at his home rather than that of the rich owner of the village because Lalo was honest and hardworking.

Guru Nanak and Sajjan Thag

One late afternoon they came to a cluster of houses where there was a **mosque** and a Hindu **mandir**. Guru Nanak decided that this was the place to stay for the night. The land owner, Sajjan **Thag**, told them that they were welcome to use the rest house which he had built for passing travellers. Later that evening Guru Nanak and Mardana began to sing some of the Guru's hymns. Sajjan listened impatiently. His mosque and mandir were really traps to catch the unwary. Guests thought that they were safe in the accommodation provided by such a godly man, but when they fell asleep he strangled them, buried their bodies and stole their belongings. Sajjan intended to do this to his two latest victims. To his annoyance they sang

ਪਹਿਲੀ ਉਦਾਸੀ ਸਮੇਂ ਸ੍ਰੀ ਗੁਰੂ ਨਾਨਕ ਦੇਵ ਜੀ ਸੁਲਤਾਨ ਪੁਰੋਂ ਚਲ ਕੇ ਐਮਨਾਬਾਦ (ਜ਼ਿਲਾ ਗੁੱਜਰਾਂ ਵਾਲਾ) ਵਿਚ ਇਕ ਗਰੀਬ ਕਿਰਤੀ ਤਰਖਾਣ ਭਾਈ ਲਾਲੋ ਦੇ ਘਰ ਗਏ ਤੇ ਭਾਈ ਲਾਲੋ ਨੂੰ ਉਪਦੇਸ਼ ਦਿੱਤਾ ਇਥੇ ਹੀ ਗੁਰੂ ਜੀ ਨੇ ਬਾਬਰੇ ਹਮਲੇਬਾਰੇ ਤ੍ਰਿਸ ਬਾਣੀ ਵਿਚ ਸ਼ਬਦ ਉਚਾਰਿਆ ਸੀ "ਜੈਸੀ ਮੈਂ ਆਵੇ ਖਸਮ ਕੀ ਬਾਣੀ ਤੈਸੜਾ ਕਰੀ ਗਿਆਨ ਵੇ ਲਾਲੋ (ਰਾਗ ਤਲੰਗ ਮਹਲਾ ੧ ਸਫਾ ੭੨੨ ਸ੍ਰੀ ਗੁਰੂਗਰੰਥਮ)

> 'Those who are true are those who are God's companions now and in the after life. The true friends will remain with God for ever but an account for all deeds will be demanded.'
>
> (GGS 729.)

Sajjan began to worry. He had committed some terrible deeds. He rushed into the room where the Guru and Mardana were and fell at Guru Nanak's feet. Could he repent? he asked. Could his life be changed? The Guru assured him that it could but he would have to pay a price. He would have to change his life and get rid of his immoral earnings. Sajjan gave his money to the poor, became one of the Guru's disciples and became the first Sikh missionary.

Guru Nanak and Dunni Chand

Not all episodes were so serious. Guru Nanak had a sense of humour and sometimes used it to make people think. One day he went to a village where a moneylender named Dunni Chand lived. Four flags flew from the roof of his house. The Guru discovered that these showed that he had four chests of treasure. He put a fresh one up whenever he filled another chest. The moneylender needed to be taught a lesson!

Guru Nanak asked Dunni Chand to look after a needle for him and return it to him when they met in the next world. Dunni Chand was pleased and impressed. The famous Guru had found him a way of serving him. Everyone likes to serve a Guru. He went home to tell his wife the good news. She was not impressed. She asked her husband how he could take anything with him when he died. The moneylender went back to the Guru, bowed in front of him and said, 'Take back your needle, there is no point in me keeping it.' 'If you cannot take this needle of mine,' said Guru Nanak, 'how can you take your treasure chests with you when you die?'

Dunni Chand gave away his possessions and became a Sikh. He followed the path which Guru Nanak taught, spending his time in meditation, working honestly and using the money which he earned to help the needy.

When he said he wished to become a Sikh, Guru Nanak told him, 'A holy person is one in whom friendship, sympathy, pleasure in helping others and a dislike of bad company are found. Good actions help us to be better people; they also contribute to the welfare of society.'

NEW WORDS

Mandir Hindu place of worship

Mosque Muslim place of worship

Thag member of a group of Indians who strangled their victims. The English word 'thug' is derived from it

Some words of Guru Arjan describing his relationship with God, the Supreme Guru.
'When I see my Guru I feel alive, my destiny, to know God, has been fulfilled.
'Hear this my prayer: bless me with your Name and make me your slave. My gracious One, keep me under your protection. With the Guru's grace a rare person understands you.
'My beloved God and friend, hear my supplication: may your lotus feet abide in my heart (i.e. may I always keep you in mind).
'Nanak offers only one prayer: may I never forget you, Treasure Store of all virtues.'

(AG 741)

6 What Guru Nanak taught

This unit tells you what Guru Nanak taught people.

The first words spoken by Guru Nanak as a religious teacher were 'Na koi Hindu, na koi Mussulman'('There is no Hindu, there is no Muslim'). This seemed very strange because at the time the Punjab was full of them! Almost everyone belonged to one or other of these two religions.

What could Guru Nanak have meant? He had been given a vision in which he believed that God had made him aware that all that mattered was knowing and serving God. If people knew God, then all the things they did, like going on pilgrimages or fasting, were worthwhile. If they didn't really know God in their hearts, these things had no meaning or value.

Guru Nanak and the village headman

Sometimes Guru Nanak was misunderstood. The khan, the headman of the village where Guru Nanak lived, was a Muslim. He was told that Guru Nanak was preaching against Islam. He ordered Guru Nanak to see him. The Guru found a Muslim religious teacher waiting for him as well as the headman. They discussed religion and then the time came for Muslim prayers. The Khan asked the Guru to join them in prayer. He went with them, but Guru Nanak did not join them in prayer. Afterwards they asked Guru Nanak to explain himself. If he was not against Islam he would surely have prayed. He shocked them by telling them that he couldn't pray with them because they were not praying! When they asked him what he meant, Guru Nanak said that the teacher's mind was not on his prayers. Back home his mare had just foaled. There was an open well in the courtyard. He had remembered that he hadn't tethered the little filly. It might have fallen down the well. Guru Nanak then turned to the khan and told him that he wasn't really praying either. His servant had been selling horses in the city of Kabul. The khan had been wondering whether he had got a good price for them. Guru Nanak reminded them that one of the most important teachings of Islam is that when anyone prays they must have the right intention, or niyat. They must be sincere and get rid of all other thoughts. Guru Nanak then said:

> 'Muslims observe five daily prayers. The first should be truth. The second purity. The third praying on behalf of others. The fourth sincere intention. The fifth virtuous actions. Those who do these things are true Muslims.'
> (AG141.)

The two Muslims agreed that Guru Nanak was a true spiritual teacher and not an enemy of Islam.

Guru Nanak and the yogi

One day Guru Nanak came to a village where he saw a man wearing only a loin cloth, sitting with his eyes shut as though he were in a trance. In front of him was a metal bowl where people placed their offerings. He was a

Handwritten copy of the Mul Mantra from the Kartarpuri Bir, the original copy of the Adi Granth. A printed version can be seen on page 47.

Hindu **yogi** who claimed to have special powers. A crowd was sitting around him. The Guru asked someone what was happening and was told that this man could see into the future. If people paid him he told them their fortunes. Guru Nanak realized that the villagers were being tricked into parting with the little money they had. Quietly, he approached the yogi, picked up his bowl and placed it behind the fortune teller's back. Then he sat down among the crowd. When the yogi opened his eyes he noticed that the bowl was missing and was very angry. He threatened that whoever had taken it would suffer terrible things. Guru Nanak then told the yogi that if he could truly look into the future he should know who had taken his bowl and where he had put it! The crowd realized that the yogi was a cheat. They grabbed the bowl and took back their money. Meanwhile the yogi thought it wise to slip away while the going was good.

The Mul Mantra

'This Being (God) is One; the truth; immanent in all things; Sustainer of all things; Creator of all things. Immanent in creation. Without fear and without hatred. Not subject to time. Beyond birth and death. Self-revealing. Known by the Guru's grace.'

These words are to be found on page one of the Sikh scriptures and on many other pages. They are often recited by Sikhs. They are said to be the first words of poetry that Guru Nanak spoke. They sum up much of his teaching. Put simply the verse teaches that there is one God, who is the Creator and present in the whole of creation. God is self-revealing; it is impossible to manipulate God or to force God to appear in some way. God is the supreme Guru, the Guru of Guru Nanak. Grace is the disclosure by God of God's love.

(Care has been taken to avoid calling God

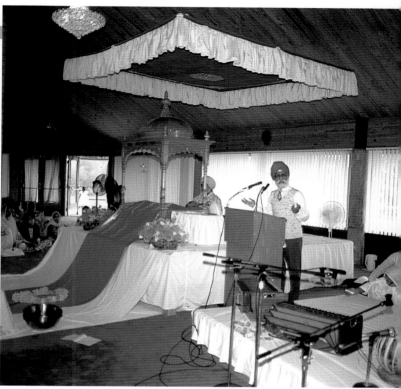
A sermon called a katha being addressed to the congregation. It will be based on the Guru Granth Sahib.

'he' or 'she', because Sikhs believe God is the Creator of male and female gender but is neither male nor female.)

NEW WORD

Yogi an ascetic who meditates

Guru Nanak sings God's praise.
'You are the source of all sound, all meditation, and absorption into your divinity. Everything that we see is your form. The senses which enjoy creation are yours. There is none other, my dear mother.
'My God is One without a second. The One sole reality. God is the destroyer and preserver, and giver of all gifts.
'God views creation, rejoices in it, and showers grace on all beings.'

(AG 350)

7 Guru Nanak, collector of hymns

This unit is about the poems of non-Sikhs which are found in the Guru Granth Sahib.

The six Gurus who composed hymns which are in the Guru Granth Sahib were:

- Guru Nanak;
- Guru Angad;
- Guru Amar Das;
- Guru Ram Das;
- Guru Arjan and
- Guru Tegh Bahadur.

The tenth Guru, Guru Gobind Singh, was also a poet, but he refused to include any of his hymns in the Guru Granth Sahib.

The Guru Granth Sahib is unusual because it also contains the writings of men who were not Sikhs. This material, known as the

bhagat bani, makes Sikhs ask two questions:

1 Who collected it?
2 Why was it put into the Sikh scripture?

Obviously the bhagat bani was arranged in the Adi Granth by Guru Arjan, but it already existed in a collection of hymns owned by one of his relatives, called Mohan. Guru Arjan borrowed it to help him in his work. The collector of most of the bhagat bani was Guru Nanak. He took a notebook with him wherever he went so that his own compositions could be recorded, as well as any others he came across on his journeys.

There is some evidence from inside the Guru Granth Sahib to support this. For example there is a poem by a Muslim called Sheikh Farid. There is also one by Guru Nanak which is similar to it but which changes some of the ideas. Obviously, Guru Nanak

Women have been important in preaching the Sikh message. Guru Amar Das is preparing them for their work in this picture.

must have known Sheikh Farid's verses. There are other places where Guru Nanak's words are rather like those of other non-Sikhs which are in the Guru Granth Sahib. It looks as though the collector of what Sikhs call the bhagat bani was Guru Nanak.

Kabir

Kabir was a famous teacher who lived at the same time as Guru Nanak but over a thousand kilometres away. There is no evidence that they ever met. Like the Sikh Gurus he taught that God was one and was pure spirit. He also believed in the importance of grace, God's loving power. He once wrote:

> 'Nothing is really done by us, what has been done is not ours. If it were, then there would be a second creator!'

Why are these hymns in the Guru Granth Sahib?

The collector of the bhagat bani didn't say that he had collected them and he didn't say why he had done it. We can offer some guesses. One reason why people often do things like this is because they haven't got enough material of their own. This cannot be the Sikh motive. Guru Nanak himself composed 974 hymns. Guru Arjan put 2218 of his own into the Guru Granth Sahib when he compiled it. Altogether the book is 1430 printed pages long! The temptation might have been to leave out the non-Sikh hymns.

Sikhs say that the reason for treasuring the bhagat bani is to show that Sikhs believe that God didn't speak only through the Gurus. God has always wanted to win the hearts of men and women, so Muslims like Sheikh Farid as well as Hindus like Namdev and Ravidas were also messengers of God. The bhagat bani shows that although Sikhs believe that their Gurus were truly teachers sent by God, there were other messengers too, who were not Sikhs.

Another reason for treasuring the bhagat bani was to create unity and tolerance among the different religious groups of North India.

NEW WORD

Bhagat bani the compositions of non-Sikhs in the Guru Granth Sahib

Some words of the famous teacher Kabir (?–c.1518).
'Wise man, answer me, what support upholds the sky? Only one who is endowed with divine wisdom may know this.'
'The sun and moon whose light spreads everywhere, these too are manifestations of the Supreme Being, Brahman (God).'
'Kabir says, this great truth may be understood only by one in whose mind God abides, and whose tongue utters God's Name.' (AG 329)

Some words of Ravidas, a poor shoemaker (?–c.1527).
'I am a lowly cobbler lacking skill, but people bring their broken shoes to me. I have no awl to pierce the holes, no knife to cut a patch. Others patch, yet they still know pain. I lack their skill, yet I know God. Ravidas repeats God's Name, thereby eluding the evil grip of death.' (AG 659)

Some words of Namdev, a low caste calico printer (c. 1270–?).
'What shall I gain if you give me a kingdom? The glory it brings is worth nothing. Why should a beggar be humiliated and scorned; why should he be treated with contempt?'
'Let me gladly give my Master praise; this is the path to bliss. Thus we are ransomed from death and transmigration. Our wanderings are brought to an end.'
'Every thing that exists, that causes doubt and delusion, is caused by your sacred plan. Only one who is granted the blessing of grace knows what it all means.' (AG 525)

8 Guru Angad

This unit describes Guru Nanak's need to appoint a successor and tells of the important work of the second Guru.

Guru Nanak's travels lasted for about 20 years. He outlived his friend Mardana, whose son, Shazada, became Guru Nanak's accompanist on his instrument, the rebeck.

Eventually Guru Nanak settled down at a Punjab village called Kartarpur on the bank of the River Ravi. Many Sikhs went there to live. Others came to listen to the Guru's teachings whenever they could. As Guru Nanak grew old he realized that he had a difficult decision to make. His disciples still needed a guide. They had the hymns which many of them knew by heart, but they needed a human teacher, too. Naturally he thought of his two sons. He decided to test them to see whether they were men who could provide the right kind of example. One day Guru Nanak let a jug fall into a muddy ditch. He asked his sons to fetch it for him. The older one, Shri Chand, refused. The filth would make him impure. The younger one thought that the task was too menial for the son of a Guru to be seen doing. Another man scrambled down the ditch without any argument; the Guru didn't even need to ask him. His name was Lehna. He had been a disciple for about nine years. Guru Nanak realized that he had found his successor.

Guru Angad

The sons were jealous of Lehna so Guru Nanak decided to let the Sikhs see clearly that Lehna had been chosen to be the second Guru. He did it in two ways. First he gave Lehna a new name, Angad. 'Ang' in Punjabi means limb, either arm or leg. Guru Nanak was saying, in a humorous way, 'Lehna is my right hand man'. Secondly, he took the canopy which was always placed over his own head as a sign of respect and put it over Angad. He placed Angad upon his own special Guru's seat, called a **gaddi**, and bowed to him. When Guru Nanak died, not long afterwards, everyone knew that they had

a new Guru, Guru Angad. The two sons left Kartarpur in disgust.

Guru Angad wrote only 62 hymns. He is better known for rearranging those of Guru Nanak and for doing something that was necessary before such a collection could be made.

Before the time of Guru Nanak there was no definite Punjabi alphabet. As an accountant he could read and write and must have felt that it was a nuisance to have no firm alphabet for his own language. He knew that Persian and Sanskrit, the languages of educated Muslims and Hindu priests, had clear alphabets. Guru Nanak used an alphabet with 35 letters in it. We know this because he composed a hymn 35 verses long. Each verse began with a different letter of the alphabet.

The Punjabi script came to be known as **gurmukhi**, which means 'from the mouth of the Guru', because it was developed by the Sikh Gurus, just as the writing used in this book is called Roman script because it was developed by the Romans. Some words using the gurmukhi alphabet can be found on page 47.

Gurmukhi is read from left to write. The words hang from the line rather than sitting on it as they do in Roman script.

It is sometimes said that Guru Angad devised the gurmukhi alphabet. The truth probably is that Guru Nanak composed it and then he and Guru Angad began to write down hymns. Until that time they would simply have been memorized. Shortly before Guru Nanak died he gave Angad a book. This may well have been a collection of Guru Nanak's hymns.

Guru Angad's task was to keep the young Sikh community going after the shock of Guru Nanak's death. People always think that such great men and women will go on forever!

Guru Angad never put his own name in his hymns. He always used the name 'Nanak' because he believed that he was continuing his teacher's work and not adding anything of his own. He was one in spirit with Guru

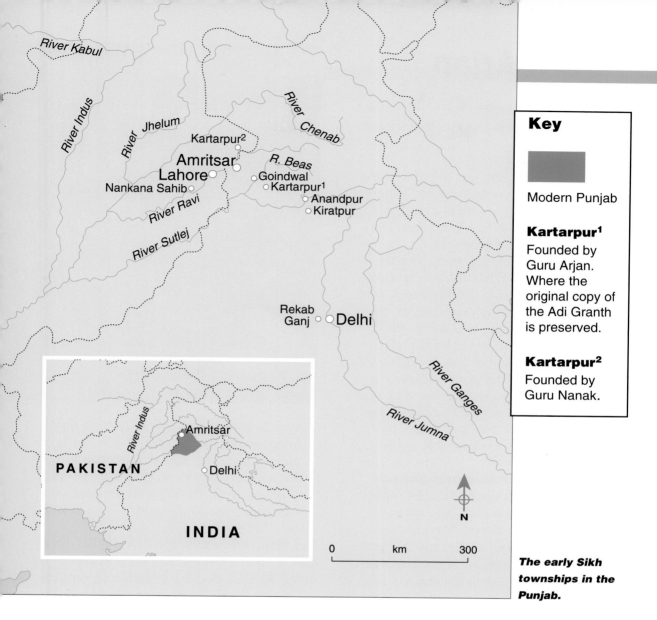

The early Sikh townships in the Punjab.

Nanak. The other Gurus who wrote hymns followed Guru Angad's example.

One of his verses seems to sum up the kind of man that Guru Angad was:

'If a servant becomes vain, quarrelsome and argumentative, he cannot earn his master's pleasure. If he serves humbly he is honoured by his master.'   (AG 474.)

NEW WORDS

Gaddi a Guru's seat

Gurmukhi the script of the Guru Granth Sahib and Punjabi

Some words from Asa-ki-Var.
Guru Nanak: 'I praise and adore my Guru (God) a hundred times a day, the One who speedily and with no delay lifts humans to the ranks of the Gods.'
Guru Angad: 'If there were a hundred moons in the heavens, if a thousand suns should shine, their light would be dim, dismal and cold, without the Guru.'   (AG 462)

19

9 Guru Arjan

This unit is about Guru Arjan and his decision to put the Sikh teachings together in a special book.

When Arjan, the man who was to become the fifth Sikh Guru, was a young man, his father sent him from Amritsar to attend a wedding in Lahore. Arjan's father was Guru Ram Das, the fourth Guru. The wedding was an important one and Arjan was sent to be the Guru's representative. While the young man was away his older brother, Prithi Chand, who had refused to obey his father and go to Lahore, got to work trying to put himself forward as the man who would be chosen to be the next Guru. His father was fit and well and not old but Prithi Chand was not a person to leave things to chance – and he was very jealous. He was sure that Guru Ram Das was preparing his 'little brother', Arjan, to lead the Sikhs, and he was probably right.

Prithi Chand's jealousy unmasked

In Indian culture it isn't usual to disobey one's parents, and it is not the custom to go to make a visit and come away when you feel like it. You wait for your hosts to say that you may go or, if your parents are more important people, you wait for them to tell you to come home.

Arjan spent some months in Lahore after the wedding and eventually decided to give his father a respectful nudge. He sent letters but his brother intercepted them and kept telling Guru Ram Das that Arjan was probably having a good time and had forgotten about his family. At last, a letter got through. It was in the form of a religious poem. Guru Arjan compared himself with the Indian pied cuckoo, the chatrik, which scurries around making a crying noise as it searches for water. These are the words which he wrote:

'My mind is filled with longing to see the Guru. It wails in tears like the chatrik. My thirst is not quenched and I will have no peace until I see him. My life is an offering to the Guru. How long must I remain separated from him? Your face brings joy. Your words bring peace. The land where you live is a blessed place. My life is an offering to my master, a sacrifice to my Guru. When shall I meet you whom I love? I shall not sleep until I am back in the Guru's court.'   (AG 96.)

Guru Ram Das was suspicious. Prithi Chand claimed that the verse was his but he had never shown a poetic inclination before. He asked him to add another couple of lines. Prithi Chand was not able to do so. The Guru then wrote to Arjan. When the young man returned he showed him the poem and asked him to complete it. Arjan wrote:

'It is my good fortune to have met the holy Guru. I have found God in my own home.'   (AG 97.)

Guru Ram Das realized which of his sons was trustworthy and fit to be the next Guru, though he probably already knew.

The need for the Adi Granth

Prithi Chand tried to start a rival movement. When his brother became Guru Arjan, he began to alter some of the Sikh hymns to make them read as though he should have

Langar. The meal is open to everyone and is therefore vegetarian. Guru Arjan stressed the importance of Langar.

been made Guru. Guru Arjan realized that the time had come to collect all the hymns which Sikhs used and put them into one book. Until then there had been several collections.

Guru Arjan had another reason for collecting all the Sikh hymns in one book and that was to meet the needs of the scattered Sikh community. The **Panth**, as Sikhs call it, was now to be found in many parts of India, hundreds of miles from the Guru. Sikhs were expected to visit him twice a year at the festival times of Baisakhi in spring and Divali in autumn, but they needed someone or something to help them in between times. There was no radio, no telephones or television in those days, of course. Letters could be sent but only if a messenger took them. There was no postal system anywhere in the world. Gurus always taught that it was the message that mattered more than the Gurus themselves. What better, then, than to make sure that every Sikh community had a copy of the Gurus' hymns!

Compiling the Adi Granth

Guru Arjan ordered all the collections that were available to be brought to him in the new town which his father had founded, Amritsar. He decided which versions were correct. He corrected errors which he found in others. Some hymns he rejected altogether, feeling that they were not by Gurus and did not contain the Sikh message. His relative, Bhai Gurdas, wrote down all the hymns, including the 2218 which Guru Arjan had composed! The task took well over a year and was completed in 1604.

At Guru Arjan's court there was a group of bards, men who composed and sang hymns. Guru Arjan included some of their hymns in the collection which he made. The collection made by Guru Arjan is called the Adi Granth. This means the first collection or first book. The Punjabi word 'adi' means first in importance, not first as in the first, second and third in a race. So Adi Granth tells Sikhs that their special book is of first class importance. It is timeless or eternal in the way that God is eternal, because it contains the word of God.

NEW WORD

Panth name of the whole Sikh community worldwide

Guru Arjan expresses the belief that God is the parent of human kind.
'You are the Supreme One, we pray to you. You have given us our being and body. You are my mother and father, we are your children.
'Many comforts lie in your grace; no one knows the limits of your glory. You are higher than the highest, the support of all creation.
'Whatever has sprung from you abides by your will. Your ways are beyond understanding, known only to yourself. Nanak, your slave is ever a sacrifice to you.' (AG 268)

This unit describes the way Guru Arjan showed his followers how important their scriptures were.

The fourth Guru, Guru Ram Das, had built a new town, Ramdaspur, which means the city of Ram Das. Today it is called Amritsar. His son, Guru Arjan, decided that this should be the place where the Adi Granth should be installed. Everyone who wished to hear it being read and meditate on its teachings could travel to Ramdaspur for that purpose.

A home for the Adi Granth

Guru Arjan's workmen erected a fine building where the Adi Granth could be placed. It stood in the middle of an artificial lake and was approached by a narrow causeway. Temples in India are usually built with one entrance which faces east towards the early morning sun. Guru Arjan's building was unusual. It had four doorways which faced north, south and west, as well as east. The reason for this was to symbolize that it should be open to men and women of all classes and to people from all directions. It had another uncommon feature. When we enter most buildings we have to climb a few steps; to enter Guru Arjan's place of worship it was necessary to go down a few steps. He said that however humble people were, they must become even more humble to enter God's house.

Sunset at the Golden Temple, Amritsar, during the Sikh festival of Divali. Bhai Budha sat under the tree in the foreground when checking the Adi Granth.

It was near this lake that Bhai Gurdas wrote down the Adi Granth. Keeping an eye on the work was a very old man called Bhai Budha. He was said to be 98 years old when the Adi Granth was finished in 1604. He had been a faithful disciple of Guru Nanak and all his successors and knew their hymns well. Guru Arjan chose Bhai Budha to be the first **granthi**. That is the name given to a person who reads and looks after the Sikh scriptures.

The place which Guru Arjan made for the Adi Granth was given the name Harmandir Sahib, the Temple of God, but Sikhs also call it the Darbar Sahib, God's Court. That is the kind of court where people gather in the presence of a king or queen, not a court of law!

When the Harmandir Sahib had been completed and the scripture carefully checked and found correct, it was installed in the new building with great rejoicing. Thousands of Sikhs were present. They watched as Guru Arjan entered the room where the scripture had been placed and saw him prostrate himself full length on the ground in front of it. He was teaching them that the words of the scripture were far more important than he was.

The survival of the Adi Granth

Since that wonderful day in 1604 Sikhs have had bad times as well as good. In 1604 the emperor who ruled the north of India, including the Punjab, was Akbar the Great, a fine, tolerant ruler. He had been shown the Adi Granth by Bhai Gurdas and Bhai Budha and was pleased with its teachings. Later, when Akbar was near Ramdaspur, he visited Guru Arjan and gave him gifts. A year later the emperor died. His successor was suspicious of Guru Arjan, who now had a large following of Sikhs. Guru Arjan was arrested and tortured to death. He became the first Sikh martyr.

The Harmandir Sahib has been damaged or destroyed about five times. Each time the Sikhs have rebuilt it. The building which people visit today was built by a Sikh ruler called Maharajah Ranjit Singh, who died in 1839. He covered so much of the building with gold leaf that it is now called the Golden Temple, in most books.

When Sikhs saw trouble coming they would move the Adi Granth to a safe place and despite every danger the original book has survived to this day. It is now in the safe keeping of a descendant of Guru Arjan in a town called Kartarpur. This is not the place where Guru Nanak lived – it is another town, near Jalandhar. The scripture is now called the Kartarpuri Bir, which means the Kartarpur book. The Kartarpuri Bir is unique. No other world religion can claim that the original copy of its scripture has survived from the day it was written down until now.

NEW WORD

Granthi person who cares for and reads the Guru Granth Sahib

At the end of the Adi Granth, Guru Arjan wrote these words.
'In this dish are placed three things; truth, contentment, and wisdom, as well as the nectar of God's Name, which is the support of everyone.'   (AG 1430)
Some other words also convey these beliefs.
'You are my Father and Mother, Kinsman and Brother. Where ever I am you are my Protector, why then should I have any fears or anxieties? By your grace I am yours.
'By meditating upon your Name I have obtained supreme bliss.
'By singing God's praises my soul is calmed.'
          (AG 103)

11 The work of Guru Gobind Singh

In this unit you will look at the importance of the last Sikh teacher, Guru Gobind Singh, who completed the Sikh scriptures.

In 1675 a disaster hit the Sikh community. Guru Tegh Bahadur, the ninth Guru, was executed on the orders of the Mughal emperor, Aurangzeb. His son, who was only nine years old, took his place. His parents named him Gobind Rai, but he later came to be called Guru Gobind Singh. This is the name by which he is best known.

The just war

Guru Gobind Singh eventually came to two important decisions. First, he decided that Sikhs should be armed and be prepared to fight, but only in a just cause. He laid down certain rules. They were:

- War should be a last resort when all efforts to settle arguments peacefully had failed.

- It should not be fought in a spirit of hatred, to gain revenge.

- There should be no looting or taking of land or property.

- The soldiers should be committed to the cause, not mercenaries, and they should not drink, smoke or molest civilians, especially women.

- The war should have clear objectives. In deciding to fight, Sikhs should not calculate the chances of success. Once the objective had been achieved fighting should cease.

Most Sikhs were farmers. The Guru had to turn them into an army. How was this to be done?

The birth of the Khalsa

At the Baisakhi harvest period on 30 March 1699 the Guru's followers gathered in his

Guru Gobind Singh and his wife Mata Sahib Kaur preparing amrit watched by the panj piare.

presence as usual, at a place called Anandpur. He told them that he needed Sikhs who would be prepared to die for their beliefs and called on them to come forward and offer him their heads. When the first volunteer was taken into the Guru's tent, not to emerge again, some Sikhs became worried. Was the Guru actually going to kill them? However, a second man followed, then a third, fourth and fifth. By this time some Sikhs had fled. Those who remained saw the Guru emerge with the five men dressed in uniform and armed. He then initiated the five men, who promised to serve him loyally, and they initiated him. The Guru called the new community which these men and women volunteered to join the **Khalsa**. This means the Pure Ones.

Khalsa vows

The Guru made them take certain vows. These were as follows. To fight if necessary, but only according to the rules he had laid down. They should not smoke, drink alcohol or commit adultery. They should meditate upon the hymns of the Gurus every morning and evening, as all other Sikhs should, but with even more devotion. They should take the name Singh, meaning lion, if they were men, and Kaur, meaning princess, if they were women. The Guru now became Guru Gobind Singh. His wife, who was also initiated, is known as Mata Sahib Kaur. Khalsa members wear the Sikh uniform.

The uniform is:

1 uncut hair (kesh);
2 a comb to keep the hair tidy (kangha);
3 a sword (kirpan);
4 short trousers (kach);
5 a wristlet worn on the right wrist, though left handed Sikhs will wear it on the left (kara).

These are called the **five Ks** because in Punjabi each begins with the initial K. Men were also instructed to wear a turban. Not all Sikhs keep the five Ks or are initiated into the Khalsa, but it is regarded as the ideal which they should reach some time in their lives.

Guru Gobind Singh told the Khalsa that he and they were one body, that his spirit lived in them.

The completion of the Adi Granth

In 1706 Guru Gobind Singh decided to complete the Adi Granth. His father, Guru Tegh Bahadur, had been inspired to compose the **gurbani** and his hymns were now included at various places in the scripture. Guru Nanak had always taught that the message which he preached mattered more than he did. Guru Arjan bowed in front of the Adi Granth when he placed it in the Harmandir Sahib in Amritsar. In that way he was saying that it was more important than

he was. Guru Gobind Singh decided that the time had come to bring the line of human Gurus to an end. It had lasted from the time that Guru Nanak began preaching in about 1499 until 1708. He would be the last.

In 1708 Guru Gobind Singh was leading his soldiers near a town called Nanded in central India. At night two men crept into his tent and stabbed him. He didn't die of his wounds immediately. The Mughal emperor, Bahadur Shah, sent his best surgeons to care for him (one was a Briton). However, the bleeding couldn't be stopped and the Guru knew that his end was near.

NEW WORDS

Five Ks the five symbols which Khalsa Sikhs must wear (males also wear a turban)

Gurbani the Sikh way of referring to the hymns of the Guru Granth Sahib

Khalsa 'the Pure Ones', a community of specially initiated Sikhs

Guru Gobind Singh recognised the presence of God in other religions, not only in Sikhism. 'God is in the Hindu temple and the mosque, in Hindu worship as well as Muslim prayer. All people are basically the same though they appear different. All have the same eyes, ears, body, and figure, made out of compounds of earth, air, fire and water. Abhekh (a Hindu name for God) and Allah are one and the same.' (Akal Ustat, Dasam Granth p.19)

12 The Guru Granth Sahib

This unit tells you how the Adi Granth became the Guru Granth Sahib, and replaced human teachers as the Sikh Guru.

When Guru Gobind Singh knew that death was near, he asked to be taken to the place where the Adi Granth was kept and bowed before it. Then he turned to the Sikhs who were with him and told them that he was dying. He said:

> 'Dear and beloved Khalsa members, the will of the immortal God can never be resisted. Whoever is born must certainly die. Henceforward the Guru will be the Khalsa and the Khalsa will be the Guru. My spirit lives on in the Khalsa and the Guru Granth Sahib.'

He opened the scripture and put some money in front of it. The Guru told the Sikhs that it would be his successor. He bowed to it, walked once around it in a clockwise direction as people often do around a Guru, and said:

> 'O beloved Khalsa, let whoever desires to see me look at the Guru Granth Sahib. Obey the Guru Granth Sahib. It is the visible body of the Guru. Let anyone who wishes to meet me search its hymns.'

He spoke with some of his closest followers for a time and then uttered his last words. He said:

The Guru Granth Sahib.
Every printed copy is 1430 pages long.

'Guru Gobind Singh obtained from Guru Nanak hospitality, the sword, victory and prompt assistance.'

Then he died. The words, which he had spoken in Persian, were later put on the coins which Maharaja Ranjit Singh issued when he became ruler of the Punjab. The Guru had said that no one should set up a memorial to him but in 1832 Maharaja Ranjit Singh ordered a gurdwara to be built where he had been cremated.

Since the death of Guru Gobind Singh the Sikhs have had no human Gurus and they never will have. The Guru Granth Sahib is the Guru. Sometimes Sikhs have needed to find out what the Guru's will is on a particular matter. If that happens they gather together in the presence of the Guru Granth Sahib, recite the prayer Ardas, and then open the scripture at random. The first verse on the left hand page will provide the guidance they need.

A gurmatta

Indian society is divided into groups based upon birth. Some are born high, for example the priests; others are born very low, such as those who skin the carcasses of animals. This division, **caste**, affects every religion in India, even though it is only really part of Hinduism. Some members of lower caste groups have become Muslim, Christian, Buddhist or Sikh to try to escape the influence of caste, but have had little success. Everyone in a village knows which group a family belongs to – their name gives them away, too. Though things are changing in India, high caste people often refuse to receive food from low caste persons. In 1920 a group of low caste converts to Sikhism in Amritsar were made members of the Khalsa. They wanted to give and receive **karah parshad** at the Golden Temple. The men in charge of it refused. Even though Sikhs believe that everyone is equal they knew that higher caste Sikhs would not eat anything touched by such men and women. There was an argument in which they were persuaded to

let the Guru decide. A copy of the Guru Granth Sahib was opened at random and these are the words which were read out:

'God gives grace to the worthless who serve the True Guru. Exalted is the service of the True Guru, brother, to hold the divine name in remembrance. We are worthless sinners but the True Guru has brought us into blissful union.' (AG 638.)

These words by Guru Amar Das persuaded the Sikhs that they had behaved badly. The converts were allowed to give and receive karah parshad.

NEW WORDS

Caste division of society into groups based on birth

Gurmatta a decision affecting the whole Sikh community reached by consulting the Guru Granth Sahib

Karah parshad a sweet mixture which Sikhs share whenever they gather for religious purposes

The Sikh Code of Conduct (Rahit Maryada) contains this teaching about reading the Guru Granth Sahib.
'Every Sikh should try to keep a place in their own home for reading and studying the Guru Granth Sahib.
'Every Sikh should read a hymn before the morning meal. If this is not possible it should be done later in the day. One should not have superstitious fears, however, if one cannot comply with this requirement. It is desirable that a Sikh should complete a full reading of the Guru Granth Sahib as often as possible.'

13 Akhand path

This unit is about special non-stop readings of the Guru Granth Sahib called **akhand paths**.

The Guru Granth Sahib is used in every part of a Sikh's religious life. Sometimes it is read from beginning to end without a break, all 1430 pages, especially at important times such as the anniversary of a Guru's birth. This reading is called an akhand path. The origin of akhand paths probably belongs to a time when Sikhs were being persecuted and had to live as nomads. Wherever they could find a place of peace they would stop and read their most precious possession, the scripture. They would be inspired by words like these:

'When a lamp is lit darkness is dispelled. Similarly, by reading religious books, the darkness of the mind is destroyed.' (AG 791.)

'The most virtuous act is that of talking about God. By listening to God's word sorrows and sufferings disappear.' (AG 265.)

Guru Amar Das said:

'Anyone can see the Guru. Mere sight does not bring spiritual liberation. This comes from meditating on the holy word.' (AG 594.)

Arranging an akhand path
The gurdwara committee plans akhand paths carefully and invites volunteers to do the reading. Those who read are men and women who must be able to intone the words properly and clearly. The intoning brings out the poetic quality of the hymns and holds the listeners' attention. There must be no mumbling, missing out words or pronouncing them incorrectly. They are reading the word of God and must do it to the best of their ability. The akhand path is usually planned to end early in the morning of the special day and is timed to last 48 hours. For example, if Guru Nanak's birthday is on 29 November, the path will begin before dawn on November 27. The relay of readers must ensure that no break occurs, so one will slide into place behind the Guru Granth Sahib as the previous reader comes to the last line of the appointed section. There will always be a reserve ready to take over in case someone is taken ill. No one should do a sitting lasting more than two hours at one time. If possible it should be less, so that the reading always sounds fresh and clear.

Preparing to read at an akhand path
The readers at an akhand path will have bathed before coming to the gurdwara. It is normal practice for a Sikh to take a bath daily anyway, but some may not be regular in this custom. No Sikh, however, would think of going to the gurdwara without bathing first. Immediately before it is their turn to read they will wash their hands to make sure that they do not soil the pages of the Guru Granth Sahib.

Attending an akhand path
Members of the **sangat**, the Sikh community, will listen to the reading when they can. It may be before going to work when the mind is fresh, or in the evening after they have bathed again to remove the grime and thoughts of their daily activities. They will try to make time in their busy lives. An akhand path gives them the opportunity to listen and meditate. Some Sikhs will sit listening for hours. Most will come during the day but some may stay for most of the night. It is unlikely that there will be a time when the gurdwara is empty except for the reader, the reserve reader and the person who gives karah parshad to worshippers.

The **langar** (meal) is served throughout an akhand path so the gurdwara committee will also have to arrange a rota of volunteers to prepare food, cook, serve and wash up. Everyone in the sangat will provide the ingredients, tea, milk and vegetables. Often a whole family will provide this service together. When the last page of the Guru Granth Sahib has been read there is a special ceremony called **bhog**, which consists of some additional verses of the scripture and the prayer Ardas.

Taking a vak. The scripture is the living word of God, so at the end of every ceremony it is opened at random to seek God's advice.

Sometimes families arrange for akhand paths to be held at special times for them like moving into a new house, or starting a new business, before a wedding, or when someone has passed examinations.

NEW WORDS

Akhand path continuous reading of the Guru Granth Sahib

Bhog ceremony at the end of an akhand path and a sadharan path

Langar meal in a gurdwara to which everyone is welcome

Sangat local Sikh community

Sikhs might remember these words of Guru Arjan when they meditate at an Akhand Path. 'Beloved devotees of God, sit with your mind concentrated on the Word. The True Guru will fulfil your tasks. God has destroyed the wicked and evil doers. The Creator has protected the honour of slaves and placed kings and emperors under their sway. I have drunk the amrit of God's Name.

'Meditate fearlessly on the Supreme One. In the company of the devout encourage others also to meditate.'

(Guru Arjan, AG 201)

14 The Guru Granth Sahib and Sikh

This unit looks at some of the moral issues dealt with by the Guru Granth Sahib.

The Gurus taught that there is one God and one humanity, so everyone should be treated with the same respect. Sikhs like to tell the story of Guru Nanak and two men called Bhai Lalo, a carpenter and Malik Bhago, who was the steward or the owner of the town of Saidpur. When Guru Nanak visited the town he took a meal with Bhai Lalo. Malik Bhago decided to hold a feast and invited Guru Nanak to be one of his guests. The Guru did not attend, which angered the steward. Guru Nanak decided that he must show Malik Bhago why he had apparently been so rude. He asked the rich man to give him a piece of bread and requested Bhai Lalo to do the same. Guru Nanak took the coarse bread of the carpenter in his right hand and the steward's dainty bread in his other. Then he squeezed them both. Blood dripped from Malik Bhago's bread and milk ran out of the other piece. The Guru said that Bhai Lalo's food was pure, the result of honest work, but Malik Bhago exploited people. That was why he had eaten Bhai Lalo's food but had refused to come to Malik Bhago's feast. Bhai Lalo became a Sikh.

Guru Nanak composed many verses about human equality. Here is one:

> 'God does not mind our caste or birth, so let us find the way of truthful living, for one's deeds proclaim one's caste and win respect.'
> (AG 1330.)

A woman distributing karah parshad. Like langar it is a way of showing equality.

ethics

Another verse says:

> 'People should be respected for the light which illumines them, not caste or birth. In the hereafter no one is regarded differently from another on grounds of caste.' (AG 349.)

There should be no **discrimination** on grounds of skin colour, race or religion, or caste. God is the creator and parent of everyone. Sikhs should always remember that Guru Nanak's closest companion was a man of low caste and a Muslim.

Women were often treated as inferior in Guru Nanak's day. He and the other Gurus said that they were as worthy of respect as anyone else. Guru Nanak said:

> 'It is from women that we are conceived and born. Woman is our life-long friend and keeps the race going. Why should we despise her who gives birth to great men?' (AG 473.)

He would have approved of the Punjabi proverb:

> 'Man builds the house; it is the woman who turns it into a home.'

In days when widows were thought to be unlucky the Sikh Gurus allowed them to remarry if they wished and said that they should be looked after by their families. Widowed and divorced Sikhs can remarry in a gurdwara. Sikhs believe that men and women should be married. It is in the human family, as we learn to love one another, that we learn to love God and realize that God cares for everyone. God has no favourites or enemies. Sikhs believe that 'charity begins at home'. That means that it is in one's home, as a child or parent, brother or sister, that we learn to be loving.

Because of the importance of the family there are no monks or nuns among Sikhs and there should be no sexual relationships outside marriage because these damage family life and trust. Bhai Gurdas, the Sikh who wrote the Adi Granth for Guru Arjan, also composed hymns. In one of them there is this sentence:

> 'A Sikh should have one wife and treat all other women as sisters, daughters or mothers.'

This also refers to Sikh wives and their behaviour towards their husbands.

Sikh conduct is summed up in these words:

> 'Nam japo, kirt karo, vand chako.'

> 'Keep God in mind always, work honestly, give to charity.'

They are the guide to the Sikh way of life.

NEW WORD

Discrimination picking on someone because of things like colour of skin or hair, accent or beliefs

Bhai Gurdas's description of the ideal Sikh.
'At dawn a Sikh awakens and practises meditation, charity and purity. A Sikh is soft-spoken, humble, benevolent, and feels grateful to others who will accept their help.
'A Sikh sleeps little, eats little, speaks little, and adopts the Guru's teaching.
'A Sikh makes a living through honest labour and gives in charity. Though highly respected a Sikh should remain humble.
'A Sikh joins the congregation morning and evening to join in hymn-singing, mind linked to the spirit of gurbani and grateful to the Guru.
'A Sikh's spontaneous devotion is selfless for it is inspired by sheer love of the Guru.'

(Var 28)

15 A Sikh wedding

This unit shows how the Guru Granth Sahib is used at a Sikh wedding.

Harbans Kaur and Jaswant Singh had not met before their parents suggested that they should marry one another. This may sound strange to many Britons but the British way of meeting, falling in love and then deciding to marry is strange to Indians. Not only Sikhs but also Hindus, Muslims, Jains, Buddhists and Christians usually have arranged marriages in India.

In the old days, when this couple's parents married, it was common for the bride and groom never to meet until the wedding itself. Now marriages are more assisted than arranged. The couple are often consulted fully and meet, though not alone, to decide whether they are happy with the partner whom their parents think would make a good husband or wife. They trust their parents, of course, because they love their children and would not like to make them unhappy.

Harbans Kaur had learned much about Jaswant Singh before she actually met him. Her father's family was related to him through marriage. Everyone was sure that it would be a good arrangement. They matched one another in so many ways; they enjoyed outdoor sports, travel, their work (she was an optician, he was a civil engineer), and both took their Sikhism seriously, going to the gurdwara regularly.

The civil wedding took place in Nottingham where Jaswant Singh's family lived, because the gurdwara in Bradford wasn't licensed for weddings. After the register office wedding Harbans Kaur went back to Bradford with her parents. Her mother said the couple were not really married, as they hadn't been to Babaji. What she meant was that they hadn't been married in the presence of the Guru Granth Sahib.

A few months later Jaswant Singh's family descended on Bradford from Canada and India, as well as from Nottingham and various parts of Britain. They were received at Harbans Kaur's home where samosas had been prepared in the hundreds, then they went to the gurdwara. Jaswant Singh was already there sitting cross-legged in front of the Guru Granth Sahib, when Harbans Kaur, with her cousin, entered and sat on his left hand side. When everyone had bowed in front of the Guru Granth Sahib and had sat down on the floor, the wedding began. A man said Ardas while the bridal couple and their parents stood. Then the granthi talked to them about the importance of marriage. He mentioned some words by Guru Ram Das,

A Sikh wedding is only valid if it takes place in the presence of the Guru Granth Sahib.

the fourth Guru, and asked them to keep them in mind always.

'Husband and wife are not two people who live together. They are husband and wife who have one spirit living in their two bodies.' (AG 788.)

The most important part was when the granthi read the **Lavan**, a hymn specially composed for weddings by Guru Ram Das. It has four verses which are spoken one at a time and then sung. As each verse is sung the couple walk around the Guru Granth Sahib in a clockwise direction, getting back to their place in front of it as the verse reaches its end. The bride followed her husband.

Here is one of the verses of the hymn:

'Our spirits find peace as the fourth round begins; for God enters our hearts and minds. By the Guru's grace we know God's presence, sweetly pervading our souls and bodies. This sweetness comes from God's love, which keeps all who speak God's name so that they may live in bliss.'

When the last circumambulation around the Guru Granth Sahib had taken place, the young couple were married in Sikh eyes. After some speeches they and then everyone else received karah parshad, left the **diwan hall** and took langar in the gurdwara's dining room.

Later that day they set out from Harbans Kaur's home to begin life in a flat in Leamington Spa, where Jaswant Singh worked. The optician that Harbans Kaur worked for had managed to transfer her to one of its branches in Coventry.

A wedding invitation showing ornate gurmukhi writing.

Some advice by Guru Arjan for newlyweds. 'Ask the happy ones how they won their beloved. They will answer, by sweetness of speech and beauty of contentment. A loaf of dry bread and a bed of bare earth is full of happiness in the company of the beloved. Let humility be the word, contentment the offering, the tongue be minted with sweet speech. Adopt these habits dear sister and he is in your power.' (AG 1384)
Guru Gobind's father told him, 'Your love for your wife should grow daily. You shouldn't be with another woman even in your dreams.' Sikh grooms are reminded of this.

NEW WORDS

Diwan hall place in a gurdwara where worship actually takes place
Lavan hymn used in a Sikh wedding. Lavan means circling

In this unit you will see that the Guru Granth Sahib is important in choosing a child's name.

It might be interesting to find out how your parents decided what you might be called. Some go to a book shop and spend weeks reading through lists of names and their meanings. Others have a family name which they choose, perhaps that of a grandparent. Sikhs have their own special way of deciding what their baby should be called.

Harbans Kaur and Jaswant Singh were thrilled when their baby girl was born. They lived in Birmingham and phoned relatives in India, Glasgow, Manchester and many other places. They also bought boxes of Indian sweets to give to neighbours and friends. Someone down the street who was not a Sikh and not familiar with Sikh ways was surprised when Jaswant Singh knocked on the door and gave him his news and the sweets. Later, when he understood, he agreed that it was a good custom. Harbans and Jaswant are modern Sikh parents; they value a daughter as much as a son. Some families only give presents if the baby is a boy, even though the Gurus said that men and women are equal and that girls and boys should be regarded as gifts from God.

During the next few days relatives brought presents. The road had never seen so many cars, especially at the weekend, when people had no need to be at work. Harbans' parents brought clothes for Harbans, and the baby. The other relatives gave money.

The baby's first visit to the gurdwara

A fortnight later, one Sunday, the baby was taken to the gurdwara to be given a name. Harbans Kaur proudly carried the baby and managed to bow to the Guru Granth Sahib while holding her. Jaswant Singh brought some coverings called rumalas to put on the Guru Granth Sahib. Other people brought cartons of milk and bags of sugar and gram flour. The congregation sang:

> 'I have the support of God, the Almighty, so my sufferings and sorrows are over. Men and women alike, rejoice. God has been good to everyone. O devotees of God, there is peace all over because God's love has spread everywhere.' (AG 628.)

Sikhs may also welcome the new member of the sangat with this hymn:

> 'God has been kind to me. The Almighty One has fulfilled my longing. I have come home purified by God's love and obtained blessing, happiness and peace. O saintly people, only God's name can give us true liberty. Always remember God and keep doing good, day and night.' (AG 621/622.)

As they sing this hymn, the parents promise to bring up their child as a Sikh so that one day, when she has become an adult, she can make her own personal commitment to God. Another popular hymn is this verse which Guru Arjan composed:

> 'Dear son, this is your mother's blessing. May God never be out of your mind even for a moment. Meditation on God should be your constant concern. It purges people from all faults. May God, the Guru, be kind to you. May you love the company of God's people. May God robe you with honour and may your food be the singing of God's praises.' (AG 496.)

Naming the baby

A Sikh stood facing the scripture and said the congregational prayer, Ardas. Then the granthi, who was a woman for this special day, asked Harbans Kaur and Jaswant Singh to bring forward their baby and lay her on the floor in front of the Guru Granth Sahib. The granthi then opened the book at random and read the first new verse on the left hand page. It began with the word 'Bishraam' from page 818, so the granthi said the baby's name should begin with 'B'. The rest of the family, who were sitting near Harbans Kaur and

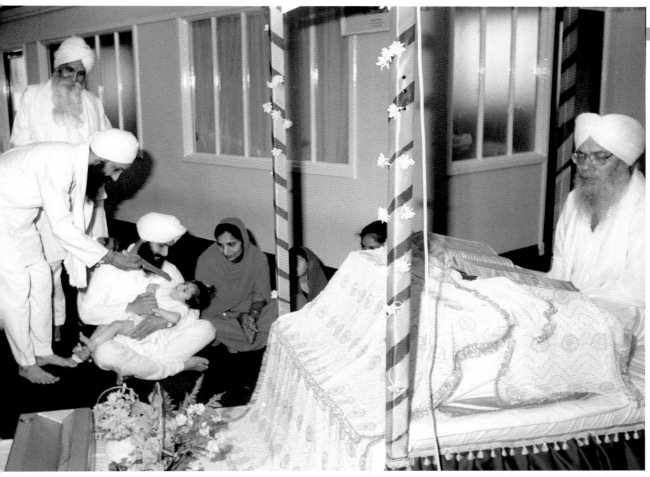

A Sikh has put some amrit on the tip of a kirpan.
This is offered to the baby during the naming ceremony.

Jaswant, spoke quietly among themselves. Balwant, Baljit, Bakshish....why not Bishraam itself (meaning peace)? Harbans Kaur realized that if she chose it she would get some peace from the relatives who were pushing their favourite names! 'Bishraam', she said. The granthi announced the name, 'Bishraam Kaur' to the sangat and added loudly, 'Jo bole so nihal' (a Sikh slogan which cannot really be translated). The congregation shouted back its agreement with 'Sat-Siri-Akal', the Sikh greeting which means 'God is truth'. Everyone shared karah parshad and friends gathered around the happy couple and the new Sikh.

Something to remember
Most Sikh names can be given to boys or girls. You can't tell if Jaswant or Harbans are male or female by looking at the name. That is why it is necessary to say 'Harbans Kaur' or 'Harbans Singh'. It is also more polite than just calling the person 'Harbans'.

This verse was composed by Guru Arjan in 1595 on the birth of his only child, a son called Hargobind, which means world-lord.
'The True Guru has sent the child, the long awaited child has been born by destiny.
'When he came and began to live in the womb his mother's heart was filled with gladness.
'The son, the world-lord's child, Gobind, is born. The one decreed by God has entered the world. Sorrow has departed, joy has replaced it. In their joy Sikhs sing God's Word.'   (AG 396)

This unit looks at the way Sikhs are comforted by the Guru Granth Sahib at the time of death.

Sikhs enjoy life as much as anyone else but the Gurus taught them that wise people should be prepared for death. This life is not the only one. We should be ready to let go of it. They said:

'The whole world is under the sway of death'
(AG 55.)

and:

'We have been born into this world with death written into our being.' (AG 686.)

We sometimes say that cars or other machines have built-in obsolescence – the manufacturer doesn't make them to last forever. Sikhs would say that human beings must realize that this is their greatest limitation:

'Whoever is born must die.' (AG 1429.)

Sikhs would say that if we have lived in union with God, death is not something to fear. It is making the union complete, undisturbed by the cares which are part of being human.

Guru Arjan said:

'When a herdsman comes to grazing land does he come to stay? Why are you so vain as to think you can stay for ever? When the time of your life is over you will have to move on. So set your affairs in order. Think of your real home. Sing God's praises and serve the Guru with love. What is there to be proud of? Like an overnight guest you must leave at dawn. Why be too attached to home and family? They are short-lived like flowers in a garden. Think of God, who provides everything that you have. Leave everything else behind.' (AG 50.)

Relatives should comfort themselves and the dying person by reciting the beautiful Sukhmani of Guru Arjan, the Hymn of Peace.

Cremation

In India the body is cremated as soon after death as possible, on the same day if this can be decently done before nightfall; otherwise the next morning. During the cremation the bedtime prayer called Sohilla is read. After all, Sikhs say, sleep is rather like death – one wakes up to something new.

The mourners then return to the gurdwara, where the granthi will read this verse, composed by Guru Tegh Bahadur:

Carrying the coffin at a funeral in Britain. In India the body is usually wrapped in a white shroud.

# of death

'Why believe that the mortal body is permanent? It passes away like a dream in the night, like the shadow of the clouds. Those who realize that the world is unreal seek protection in God.'   (AG 219.)

Two hymns, called Ghorian, by Guru Ram Das (AG 575) and Alahunian, by Guru Nanak (AG 578 to 582) are also often sung. Part of Alahunian reads:

'You are Father, Mother and Friend, Cherisher of the world. The whole world is your child. Whoever seeks you as refuge obtains a treasury of merits and does not suffer rebirth. By keeping God in mind night and day we get our heart's desire.'

Remembering the dead

During the following week the family of the deceased will probably arrange for the Guru Granth Sahib to be read in their home. This will not be a continuous, unbroken reading because they have to return to their daily work. It will be read early in the morning and especially in the evening. It is called a **sadharan path**. It keeps them occupied and helps them to find comfort during the period of greatest grief.

Sikhs do not put up gravestones or monuments to the dead. They are taught that they should be honest and helpful in their dealings with one another throughout their lives and that the memory of their goodness is the only memorial that they need. Guru Nanak said:

'The dead keep their link with the living through the memory of their good deeds.'
(AG 143.)

The ashes of a Sikh may be thrown into any canal or river. Sometimes in Britain, where this is forbidden, they are taken some miles out to sea. In India they may be taken to a town called Kiratpur, in the Punjab, where the remains of Guru Hargobind were put in the river. Some British Sikhs will take the ashes

Paying final respects before cremation.

there too, but it is the soul's journey that matters and not what happens to the body's remains.

NEW WORD

Sadharan path a non-continuous reading of the Guru Granth Sahib

Words from Alahunian.
'Friends, pray for my union with the Beloved, a union which can never be broken. Bless me, so that I may serve God lovingly. Some have strayed from the path of serving God. Warn them to return to it instead of treading the path of death. Through good fortune we meet friends and relations who have met the Guru and so slipped out of death's noose.'
(AG 582)

This unit looks at how the scriptures are used in the initiation of Sikhs into the Khalsa.

The story of the beginning of the Khalsa was told in Unit 11. Ever since that time Sikhs have been encouraged to follow the example of the **panj piare**, Guru Gobind Singh and his wife Mata Sahib Kaur. Not all of them do, often because they do not think that they can live up to the standard which membership demands. The Khalsa vows can be difficult to keep.

Amrit pahul, which is the Sikh name for the initiation ceremony, must take place in the presence of the Guru Granth Sahib. A copy will be taken to the room which has been prepared. It cannot be held in the main hall of the gurdwara during a service because public worship is open to anyone, including non-Sikhs. Those who conduct the ceremony must be **amritdhari**, which means they must have been initiated. They will be wearing the five Ks. Seven people are needed for the ceremony. One acts as granthi, sitting behind the Guru Granth Sahib, and five are the panj piare. The seventh person is there to make sure that there are no interruptions. Of course, women as well as men may conduct amrit pahul. The people who are going to become Khalsa Sikhs will also wear the five Ks. They are asked if they wish to be initiated. When they have said that they do, they are told what it means to be a member of the Khalsa by being reminded what Guru Gobind told his followers in 1699. Then the ceremony begins.

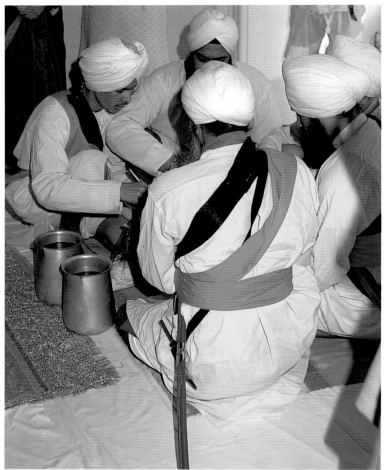

The panj piare preparing amrit. Compare this picture with the one on page 24.

The amrit ceremony

The Guru Granth Sahib is opened at random and a passage is read out. Then comes the prayer, Ardas, after which the panj piare pour water into a steel bowl and keep adding sugar crystals to it. This is the **amrit**. They stir the liquid and recite some hymns at the same time. The hymns are:

- the Japji of Guru Nanak;

- the **Jap** of Guru Gobind Singh;

- ten verses called Swayyas, by Guru Gobind Singh;

- Chaupai, another collection of verses by Guru Gobind Singh;

- six verses from the Anand, which was composed by Guru Amar Das.

ceremony

These are hymns which Sikhs should use every day in meditation so the panj piare and the initiates should know them well.
Here are a few verses from each of the passages used in amrit pahul:

'When the hands, feet and body are covered with dust the dirt is removed by washing them with water. Filthy clothes can be washed clean with soap. But the mind which has been soiled by evil thoughts can only be made clean by loving God's name. Virtue and vice are not mere words. We carry the effects of our deeds with us. Whatever seed is sown, the same fruit is reaped. Birth and death are decided by God.'   (Japji AG 4.)

'God has no marks or symbols, no colour or caste, no family line. No one can describe God's form, hue, features or attire. God is eternal, self-enlightened and of infinite power.'   (Jap, verse 1.)

'Mighty elephants in gorgeous array, magnificently decked out in gold; thousands of horses nimbler than deer, swifter than the wind; their masters are powerful emperors before whom countless people bow. In the end such greatness crumbles to nothing as they go on their way.'   (Swayya 3.)

'God knows how everyone feels in their heart, what troubles good people and bad. From the ant to the elephant, we are all under God's kind eye.'   (Chaupai 11.)

'O my mind, concentrate on God, stick to God! Your sufferings will vanish. If God accepts you you will succeed. God is almighty and can do anything for you, so why forget God? O my mind, stay fixed on God always.'   (Anand AG 917.)

When the amrit is ready some of it is poured into the cupped hands of each initiate for them to drink. This is done five times. Then it is sprinkled on their eyes and hair, again five times. Each time they say 'Vahiguruji ka

Khalsa, Vahiguruji ki fateh!' 'Hail to the Khalsa, victory belongs to God!'

If there is any amrit left the initiates all drink it from the bowl.

The final part of the service is the recitation of the Mul Mantra, and giving Sikh names to any converts. Then everyone in the room shares karah parshad from the same bowl.

NEW WORDS

Amrit the liquid used in the initiation ceremony. Can also mean nectar

Amritdhari a Sikh who has been initiated into the Khalsa

Amrit pahul the Khalsa initiation ceremony

Jap opening hymn of the Dasam Granth

Panj piare the first five men to become Khalsa members; the five people who perform the initiation ceremony (they may be made up of men and women)

Six verses of the Anand, The Hymn of Bliss, composed by Guru Amar Das, are recited during the preparation of amrit. Here is one of them.
'The true Name is my support.
'It is my food and drink; by it my hunger of every kind is removed.
'By saturating my mind, it has satisfied all my longings and given me peace and happiness.
'Such are the excellencies of my Guide, at whose feet I wish to pour out my life for ever and ever.
'You too should love God's word, O my kin in spirit! It is the support of my life.'
'The manifold strains of its music resound in the heart that is blest;
'Aye, blessed is the heart that, touched by grace, vibrates with the Name.'

This unit describes some of the ways in which Sikhs use the Guru Granth Sahib besides worship.

The Guru Granth Sahib in the home

Many Sikh families keep a complete Guru Granth Sahib in their homes. If they do, they must take great care of it. It should be given its own room. They often call it Babaji's room. 'Baba' is a respectful and affectionate word which can be used when reference is being made to a Guru or an elderly member of the village. It means father. If a family does own a copy of the Guru Granth Sahib someone should get up before dawn, take a bath, open it and read it. Before going to bed they should read it before closing it for the night. Many families sit together when the children have finished their homework to enjoy a time of meditation.

Sikhs who cannot give the Guru Granth Sahib the respect and care it needs may decide to keep a **gutka** instead. This is not much larger than a pocket diary. It contains the verses which Sikhs read or recite and meditate on every day. (They are the same as the ones used in the amrit ceremony in Unit 18.) When it is not being used it should be wrapped in cloth, perhaps in a clean handkerchief, and kept in a special place such as the top bookshelf. Sikhs will wash their hands before opening it and may kiss the gutka to show respect and affection.

Many religious people say grace before eating food. Sikhs may say some words of Guru Arjan:

> 'God is the only giver whose treasures and gifts are limitless. How can I begin to praise the one who gives me all that I have? We are nursed like children, constantly in God's care. We can never know all of God's wonders. Only those who learn what God teaches can experience true happiness.'   (AG 957.)

At the end of the meal they may say:

> 'O God, we have enjoyed food from your treasure store. We thank you for it. Through Guru Nanak may the glory of your name increase and may the whole world be blessed by your grace.'

The Guru Granth Sahib outdoors

In Punjab, where much of the year is hot and dry, most of life is lived outdoors. Weddings sometimes take place on the top of a flat-roofed house or in the garden, if they are big enough. When this happens the Guru Granth Sahib is carried from the gurdwara or Babaji's room on someone's head and another person walks behind waving the chauri. The Guru Granth Sahib will be placed on its stool, the manji sahib, and cushions, and a canopy will be put over it, just as in the gurdwara (see Unit 1).

Changing the cover (chola) of the Nishan Sahib at Baisakhi.

Nagar kirtan. The lorry carries a copy of the Guru Granth Sahib.

Nagar kirtan

Festivals are celebrated in the open air in India. Baisakhi in April, Divali in October and even Guru Nanak's birthday in October or November are times when it is nearly always sunny. In towns a lorry will be decorated with bunting and flowers and the Guru Granth Sahib will be put on it, with a number of young Sikhs dressed in white and wearing the five Ks. Children dressed in school uniform may walk in front of the float or behind it. Bands will lead the procession but in front of them will be five people, the panj piare. They, too, will be dressed in white except for orange or blue turbans and sashes. They walk barefoot and carry flags. Other Sikhs may be in the long procession. Many will stand at the roadside or look from upstairs windows, watching it pass by. This procession is called **nagar kirtan**. Nagar means town, and kirtan means songs of praise.

Sikhs have begun to celebrate Baisakhi with nagar kirtan in some British towns and cities, such as Southall, Leeds and Leicester. It will usually be held on the Sunday following 13 April, the date of Baisakhi.

NEW WORDS

Gutka a small book containing the main hymns used in daily meditation

Nagar kirtan a procession of the Guru Granth Sahib led by the panj piare

The religious duties of a Sikh.

'I bow to those Sikhs who wake up at dawn for meditation and who bathe early in the morning.

'I bow to those Sikhs who recite the Holy Name with concentration.

'I bow to the Sikhs who walk to participate in the congregation and who sing or listen to the Guru's hymns daily.

'I bow to those Sikhs who find good Sikhs and befriend them.

'I bow to those Sikhs who perform sincere worship and celebrate the Sikh festivals. By serving the Guru, their lives become fruitful and blessed.' (Bhai Gurdas)

This unit is about the writings of Guru Gobind Singh, Bhai Gurdas and Bhai Nand Lal.

The Dasam Granth

In 1706 Guru Gobind Singh took a copy of Guru Arjan's Adi Granth and ordered one of his followers, Bhai Mani Singh, to add the 116 hymns of the ninth Guru, Guru Tegh Bahadur, to it. He didn't put any of his own compositions into it even though he was a great poet. The Guru was a highly educated man. He knew Persian, Sanskrit, which was the ancient sacred language of India, and Hindi. In his verses he used all of them.

After Guru Gobind Singh's death Bhai Mani Singh collected the tenth Guru's writings. He finished this task in 1734. Bhai Mani Singh was born in 1644 and had known the last four Gurus. He had been a close companion of Guru Gobind Singh and his father Tegh Bahadur and was a respected preacher and teacher of the Guru Granth Sahib. Guru Gobind Singh gave him the task of looking after the Harmandir Sahib and the services which were held there every day. He was clearly the best man to collect together what the tenth Guru had written. The collection of Guru Gobind Singh's writings is called the **Dasam Granth**, the Book of the tenth Guru. One printed version is 1428 pages long.

One composition was a letter to the Mughal emperor, Aurangzeb. Guru Gobind Singh believed that his treatment of his Hindu and Sikh subjects was unjust. He fought the emperor's army and sent Aurangzeb a letter in Persian, the language of the royal court. It is called Zafarnama, or Letter of Admonition. Admonition means telling someone off! Guru Gobind Singh told the emperor that his subjects had a right to fight against him if he did not treat them

A portrait representing the mystical union of Guru Nanak, Guru Gobind Singh and the Guru Granth Sahib.

writings

justly. This is one of the sentences which he wrote:

> 'I had to fight the invading army with arrows and guns because when all peaceful means have been tried and do not succeed it is lawful to make use of the sword.'

The hymn which Bhai Mani Singh placed first in the Dasam Granth is called the Jap, which means recitation. Sikhs should recite it every morning. A few lines from it are quoted in the unit on the amrit ceremony (Unit 18). Another is called **Akal Ustat**, The Praise of the Eternal One. Part of it reads:

> 'Humanity is one race in the whole world. God as Creator, as bountiful and as merciful is One God. We should never try to divide God into the God of different groups. Worship the One God, the One Divine Teacher of everyone. Everyone has the same human form, everyone has the same soul.'

The Dasam Granth is never installed in gurdwaras or carried in processions and most Sikhs only know the passages which should be meditated upon every day plus a few famous lines such as the ones written above, but in theory it is one of the sacred books of the Sikhs.

There are two other Sikhs whose writings may be recited in gurdwaras.

Bhai Gurdas

Bhai Gurdas (born between 1560 and 1580, died 1633) was a nephew of Guru Amar Das, who instructed him in the Sikh faith. Guru Ram Das sent him to the town of Agra to be a missionary. Guru Arjan decided that he was the man to compile the Adi Granth in 1604 under the Guru's guidance. He was a great poet and a very able scholar but none of his poems were included in the Adi Granth. It is said that Guru Arjan thought he was already conceited enough! Nevertheless everyone admits that he was probably the ablest Sikh, next to the Gurus themselves, and so his

writings may also be used in gurdwaras. They are often described by Sikhs as the key to the Guru Granth Sahib. He was so much respected that Sikhs gave him the title 'Bhai', meaning brother.

Bhai Nand Lal

Nand Lal (1633–about 1712) was a scholar and poet in the Persian and Arabic languages. He married a Sikh, met Guru Gobind Singh and eventually became one of his followers. He was also the tutor of Bahadur Shah, the son of the emperor Aurangzeb. In 1708 Nand Lal was among Guru Gobind Singh's companions when the Guru was assassinated. Because he wrote in Persian his works are seldom read in gurdwaras, but they could be. He was also honoured with the title 'Bhai'.

NEW WORDS

Akal Ustat hymn composed by Guru Gobind Singh

Dasam Granth collection of the compositions of the tenth Guru

Guru Gobind Singh describes the purpose of his life.
'For this purpose God sent me.
Then I was born and came into this world.
I tell you what God told me;
I have no enmity with any one.
Those who call me God
Will fall into the pit of Hell.
Regard me as a servant of the Lord.
Do not have any doubt about it.
I am the slave of the Supreme Being;
I have come to witness the world-drama;
I tell the people what God told me then;
I shall not keep silent on account of the fear of mortals.'

This unit explains why the Golden Temple is an important place for Sikhs.

Sikhs don't believe in pilgrimages. They say that God is everywhere so there is no need to go to special places. The only journey needed is an inner one to find God, who lives within each one of us. However, there is one place which holds special affection for Sikhs. It is the Golden Temple in the city of Amritsar. It is really a gurdwara with four entrances, set in the middle of a rectangular artificial lake. High walls with shops set into the side of them separate it from the streets of Amritsar. You climb down a few steps, pass through an open gateway and there is the Golden Temple, shining in the bright sun. It is a wonderful sight! Thousands of Sikhs go there every day and Sikhs from Britain try to visit it when they go to stay with relatives in India.

Inside the Golden Temple

Because the whole Golden Temple area is special you must cover your head and walk barefoot even outdoors along the **parkarma**, the marble pavement which runs all the way around the pool. Whichever entrance you enter by you must also turn left, in a clockwise direction, keeping the Golden Temple on your right hand side. Eventually you reach the footbridge from the parkarma to the gurdwara proper. It has two walkways divided by railings. People enter by the left one and leave by the right. It helps the crowds to move more easily. Inside the gurdwara is a copy of the Guru Granth Sahib, which is read in the early morning. Singing of kirtan then continues all day till long after it is dark. The reading and chanting is amplified by microphones so that it can be heard wherever you are in the Golden Temple area or even walking along the streets outside.

Removing and returning the scripture

Late at night the Golden Temple is closed. The great doors are shut from 10.30 p.m. until 2.30 a.m. so that the premises can be cleaned. Just before they are closed the Guru Granth Sahib is closed, wrapped up and put onto a palanquin called a **palki** by the Sikhs, to be carried on their shoulders to the room called the **Kotha Sahib** in the Akal Takht, a building across the causeway where it will spend the night. Crowds gather for sukh asan and Sikhs vie with one another to hold one of the four poles which support the palki. Non-Sikh visitors may be lucky – they may be invited to join the procession and room will be made for them to hold one of the poles for a few metres of the Guru Granth Sahib's journey.

Soon after 2.30 a.m. singing resumes in the gurdwara. A crowd gathers at the door of the building in which the Guru Granth Sahib lies. When it is brought out to be put back into the palki they shower it with flowers and small pieces of perfumed cotton wool and again try to catch hold of the poles holding the palki to carry the scripture back to the gurdwara. A granthi follows waving a chauri. Behind him come musicians, one of them blowing a long trumpet, and then members of the sangat chanting hymns. One verse might be:

The visitor's first sight of the Golden Temple on entering by one of the gateways.

Golden Temple

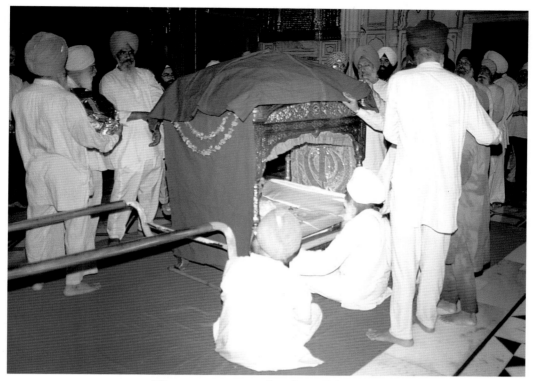

Three a.m. – preparing the palki to carry the Guru Granth Sahib.

'Others have someone to lean on but you, O God, are my only support. I would writhe in pain if you did not dwell in my heart. I remember you in good times and in bad. This is the way to seek God, says Nanak.'

(AG 791.)

At the entrance to the gurdwara the palki is put down. The granthi lifts the Guru Granth Sahib from it with great respect, carries it inside and lays it on the manji sahib. By now all singing has stopped and there is complete silence for the Sikh prayer, Ardas. Then the scripture is opened at random so that its advice for the day can be discovered. (Later someone will put this on a notice board for worshippers who come later in the day.) Karah parshad is distributed. Kirtan, the singing of hymns, resumes and the busy life of the Golden Temple has begun again.

NEW WORDS

Kotha Sahib room where the Guru Granth Sahib is kept when not in use

Palki Punjabi name for the palanquin which carries the Guru Granth Sahib at the Golden Temple

Parkarma pavement around the pool at the Golden Temple

Guru Arjan composed Sukhmani, 'The Pearl of Peace'. It begins:
'Turn to God in contemplation; in calling God to mind find peace. Thus our inner turmoil is stilled and all anguish driven away. Behold the glory of the earth's Sustainer. Those who repeat God's praise are numberless. The hallowed pages of scripture are but a syllable of what the Name contains. Those who receive a glimpse of its meaning will earn a glory which none can describe. With those who seek that glimpse, O God, your slave Nanak finds release.' (AG 262)

22 Printed copies and translations

This unit is about the change from handwritten copies of the Guru Granth Sahib to printed versions.

When Bhai Gurdas compiled the Adi Granth supervised by Guru Arjan, it was written by hand. Copies were made and when Bhai Mani Singh wrote the final version in 1706, adding the hymns of Guru Tegh Bahadur, this was also a manuscript. It must have taken many months of patient hard work to produce a single copy. Printing wasn't needed in Punjab until the 19th century. There was little need for writing at all outside the Mughal court and there were plenty of people who were eager to earn their money keeping the few account books that were necessary. In those days farmers didn't need to fill in forms and few people wrote letters. They didn't move away from home as they do now. Families lived in the same village for centuries. Sikhs didn't have relatives in Britain or the USA to write to! Memories were good. Most Sikhs could remember the hymns of the Gurus, or at least those which they used every day. Many still know them by heart today. The only need for writing was to provide scattered Sikh communities with their own copies of the scriptures. To copy them was a great honour and a labour of love.

The coming of the westerners

Things began to change in 1834 when an American Christian missionary came to the Punjab town of Ludhiana. Printing presses were introduced to produce copies of the New Testament. Mission schools were set up and missionaries also toured the villages preaching the Christian message. Some Sikhs converted to Christianity. Hindus belonging to an organization called the Arya Samaj began working in the Punjab too. They wanted

to convert Sikhs to their form of Hinduism. Sikhs felt threatened and decided that the best way to resist these pressures was to use the methods of their opponents. Colleges and schools known as Khalsa colleges were established. The printing press was used to provide copies of the Guru Granth Sahib which were cheap in price compared with the handwritten editions. Thousands could be printed in less time than it took to copy one manuscript version.

The use of printed Guru Granth Sahibs in gurdwaras

Today all printed copies of the Guru Granth Sahib are identical and are 1430 pages long. You can find them in every gurdwara. But this has not always been the case. The first copies were put into five volumes and Sikhs were told that they should not be rebound to form one book. This was to stop them being installed in gurdwaras. After strong debate, however, single volume copies were printed and installed and the anxieties of the traditionalists were shown to be groundless. No book in the world can be treated more reverently than the Guru Granth Sahib, even

Three a.m. at the Golden Temple. Waiting for the Guru Granth Sahib to be brought from its resting place to the palki.

in its printed form. A number of publishers produced copies and it was not until the early 20th century that the 1430-page edition won acceptance over its rivals.

Transliterations of the Guru Granth Sahib

A transliteration is changing the alphabet of one language and replacing it with another. (It isn't a translation, which is when the words of one language are replaced with those of another.) Codes sometimes work this way, or you may have written down some Viking runes and then written the Roman letters which we use for writing English underneath them. Here are some Punjabi words.

ਗੁਰੂ ਨਾਨਕ

ਗੁਰੂ ਗਰੰਥ ਸਾਹਿਬ

The English transliteration of them reads:

Guru Nanak

Guru Granth Sahib

Transliterations were made in Hindi and Urdu to help people who could speak Punjabi but wrote in the Hindi and Urdu scripts. Many Sikhs did in the early 20th century, but today most speak and write Punjabi using the gurmukhi script.

Translations of the Guru Granth Sahib

Westerners became interested in Sikhism in the 19th century and scholars translated parts of the Guru Granth Sahib into English. It was not until 1961 that a complete translation was made. The poet Dr Gopal Singh was the man who produced it. Dr Jarnail Singh, a Sikh living in Canada, has made a French translation.

Plans are in hand for a group of Sikhs to produce a modern translation in the kind of English which is used today. There are many young Sikhs living in Britain and North America who cannot read the Guru Granth Sahib in the original. Sikhs also believe that

ਜਪੁ ਜੀ ਸਾਹਿਬ

ੴ ਸਤਿਨਾਮੁ ਕਰਤਾ ਪੁਰਖੁ ਨਿਰਭਉ ਨਿਰਵੈਰੁ ਅਕਾਲ ਮੂਰਤਿ ਅਜੂਨੀ ਸੈਭੰ ਗੁਰ ਪ੍ਰਸਾਦਿ ॥ ॥ ਜਪੁ ॥ ਆਦਿ ਸਚੁ ਜੁਗਾਦਿ ਸਚੁ ॥ ਹੈ ਭੀ ਸਚੁ ਨਾਨਕ ਹੋਸੀ ਭੀ ਸਚੁ ॥੧॥ ਸੋਚੈ ਸੋਚਿ ਨ ਹੋਵਈ ਜੇ ਸੋਚੀ ਲਖ ਵਾਰ ॥ ਚੁਪੈ ਚੁਪ ਨ ਹੋਵਈ ਜੇ ਲਾਇ ਰਹਾ ਲਿਵ ਤਾਰ ॥ ਭੁਖਿਆ ਭੁਖ ਨ ਉਤਰੀ ਜੇ ਬੰਨਾ ਪੁਰੀਆ ਭਾਰ॥ ਸਹਸ ਸਿਆਣਪਾ ਲਖ ਹੋਹਿ ਤ ਇਕ ਨ ਚਲੈ ਨਾਲਿ ॥

A printed copy of the Mul mantra.

the message that the Gurus preached should be available to as many people as possible. Their spiritual riches should be shared with everyone. Work has only just begun. It may be completed in 1999, in time for the 300th anniversary of the founding of the Khalsa.

Bhai Gurdas sums up what it means to be a Sikh.
'Learning Sikhism implies linking one's consciousness to the Holy Word, learnt in the company of holy people.
'Sikh meditation implies drinking the nectar-like juice of the Guru's mantra.
'The fragrance of Sikhism is like the sweet smell of the sandal tree which can be experienced at a distance.'
'Its realisation is humble acceptance of the Holy Name and losing one's identity in it.
'Its practice is listening to the hymns of the Guru in the congregation with devotion, practising meditation, and doing good works.'

Index